Jesus can heal anything

if you believe...

believe that God take control of your life with your whole heart

trust Him with it no matter what...

what life might be like if circumstances were different

the totality of the life that has been given us

a gift of encouragement

FOR

FROM

DATE

Beyond the Sorrow

There's Hope
in the Promises of God

TAMMY TRENT

Nashville, Tennessee

Project Editor: Pat Matuszak

Project Manager: Kathy Baker

Designed by Koechel Peterson & Associates, Minneapolis, Minnesota

The LORD *is close to the brokenhearted,*

and he saves those whose spirits

have been crushed.

PSALM 34:18 NCV

The Lord Is Near to the Brokenhearted

This story is not just my life's story. All who risk loving, risk losing the one they love. Sometimes that loss comes through death of the one we love, other times love itself seems to have died when a relationship is broken. In every loss, we have to look to the very source of love, to Jesus Christ, for strength to keep pressing on. He has given us precious promises in His Word to bring the pieces of our lives back together. The Bible is like an eternal love letter that will give us hope through all of life's trials and unite our hearts with His.

I've just made it through the hardest weekend of the year for me—the anniversary of the day I lost my husband, Trent, in a diving accident. As a young married couple, we thought we'd have a long lifetime to grow old together. We had just begun to talk about starting a family when he was taken from me. If you could see me sitting here, you'd see a woman who's still very broken. I must admit, there are still days when all I want to do is close the window shades and curl up on the couch praying that I'll wake up from this unbelievable dream that my life has become. I've traveled through grief and sorrow, and God keeps calling me to a new place, to take a step—just one step at a time—that will take me beyond the sorrow into His joy.

BEYOND THE SORROW

His Invitation

One of the most important choices anyone can make in life is to keep living, no matter what circumstances surround you. It is never hopeless when you know the Lord, when you know who God really is—not some figure up on a throne, but someone who loves you and wants to have a personal relationship with you. Knowing we are not alone and that we will be comforted is what helps us make it through. God is still good when life is hard. And His invitation to choose life is always there for us.

. . . *choose life,*

> *that both you and your descendants may live;*
>
> *and that you may love the* LORD *your*
>
> *God, that you may obey His voice,*
>
> *and that you may cling to Him,*
>
> > *for He is your life . . .*

DEUTERONOMY 30:19, 20 NKJV

HIS INVITATION

My Choice: To Say Yes!

I'd always been taught that God has a plan for my life. I truly believed that it was an adventurous plan, filled with life and love and a relationship with God. I didn't create my husband, God did. And He didn't create Trent to fulfill my plans, He created Trent to fulfill His plans. Ultimately, that means we are living out God's will, not our own, and at the end of our life's story He will be glorified.

"I have good plans for you," says the LORD. *"I have good plans for you, not plans to hurt you. I will give you hope and a good future."*

JEREMIAH 29:11 NCV

I had to live out that belief in God's plan when tragedy struck. God had been part of my life since I was a child, but sometimes it seemed like I was praying to someone who lived on a big throne in heaven, not sitting next to me on my couch. But His presence has become so real to me since I lost Trent. I had to just depend on Him in a close, personal way. And He has met me there. He has kept His promise to give me strength to carry on through the dark days, comfort me with His love, and lead me back home.

I was sent to help the faith of God's chosen people and to help them know the truth that shows people how to serve God. That faith and knowledge come from the hope for life forever, which God promised to us before time began. And God cannot lie.

TITUS 1:1, 2 NCV

Drawing Near

When I first lost my husband, it seemed impossible to even breathe. Shock, then sadness, and sometimes fear, literally took my breath away. But God's healing came into my life one day, one step, and even one breath at a time. Today, I am not only breathing again, I am dancing. Connie Neal wrote a book called *Dancing in the Arms of God* to describe how it felt to follow the Lord through life's difficulties. At first, I could not imagine ever dancing again. Ever being that happy. It was a struggle just to sit up and get out of bed. But I could feel the very presence of God reaching out to me. I could sense the prayers of my family and friends when I couldn't pray myself. There was hope in that for me.

*Draw near to God
and He will draw near to you.*

JAMES 4:8 NKJV

When you draw near to God in times of trouble,
you learn who He really is. Then you learn:

- ❧ You can trust Him.
- ❧ He is not sitting in heaven on a throne,
  but walking with you here on earth.
- ❧ He wants a personal relationship with you.
- ❧ You can know the depth of His love for you.
- ❧ Your soul craves relationship with God.
- ❧ You can call on Him for help *first*, not after
  other sources have failed.

Dancing Like
No One Is Watching

I love these thoughts I heard from my very good friend Luci Swindoll:

"Work like you don't need the money. Love like you've never been hurt. Dance like no one is watching, and live like it's heaven on earth."

Sometimes all we want is a safe path with no risks. But you can't dance if you don't risk standing up and trying to take a step forward. You can't live if you don't take any chances either. We need to say yes to life, even if we can't control the outcome of our life's story. Be brave. Choose to live and to embrace your life with joy.

> *"Then you will call my name.*
> *You will come to me and pray to me,*
> *and I will listen to you.*
> *You will search for me.*
> *And when you search for me with all your heart,*
> *you will find me! I will let you find me,"*
> *says the LORD.*
> JEREMIAH 29: 12–14 NCV

FAITH

Faith is a risk, but not having faith is also a risk. We risk missing out on our lives becoming a part of the greatest love story of all time— the story of a God who loved us so much that He left heaven to be with us.

"God loved the world so much
that he gave his one and only Son
so that whoever believes in him
may not be lost,
but have eternal life.
God did not send his Son
into the world
to judge the world guilty,
but to save the world through him."

JOHN 3:16, 17 NCV

IS A RISK

Give and Take Rhythm

Maybe we want a quick push-button fix for every difficulty. Our modern world is like that: three steps to solve every problem from fitness to relationships. But Jesus never said life would be easy—He just promised that He wouldn't leave us alone. So in the midst of our problems, we are not alone even when we are the only ones in the room. We feel His presence and strength when we pray.

"If ye love me, keep my commandments.
And I will pray the Father,
and he shall give you another Comforter,
that he may abide with you for ever;
even the Spirit of truth;
whom the world cannot receive,
because it seeth him not,
neither knoweth him:
but ye know him;
for he dwelleth with you,
and shall be in you.
I will not leave you comfortless:
I will come to you."

JOHN 14:15–18 KJV

God also sends people to comfort us so we will know He has heard our call for help. We can ask for guidance to wisely discern which people have been sent by God to affirm us and speak strength into our lives. We need to invite those people into relationship and nurture those ties. I purposely gathered a circle of supportive friends around me just to hang out. I called them when I needed help, because I could trust that they meant what they said when they promised to be there for me. After they had been so faithful to help me, I wanted to give something back. I invited a core group of friends to come to my home for dinner regularly. I needed to be able to give back even in my own loss. There was strength in receiving help and strength in giving something back.

"Give, and you will receive.
    You will be given much.
Pressed down, shaken together,
    and running over, it will spill into your lap.
The way you give to others
    is the way God will give to you."

LUKE 6:38 NCV

A Surprise Partner

Sometimes God answers our prayers by sending people to rescue us who we haven't asked for help.

One day I was working in my yard trying to trim a branch off of a tree. It was a tree that Trent gave me for my birthday in April 2001, and I didn't want to ruin it; but I didn't have a strong enough saw to cut through the entire branch. I sat down there and cried. I missed my husband so much at that moment. He would have known what to do and how to take care of it for me.

"I hate this!" I yelled at God. "This is what my life is going to be like from now on, isn't it?" I felt so frustrated and so out of control.

Suddenly, a neighbor lady pulled up in her car and saw that I needed help.

"Tammy, you need a chainsaw? Wait a minute." I watched her pull into her driveway and could hardly keep from laughing as the little woman came out of her garage toting a full-size chainsaw.

"I just had this hanging on my wall," she explained. She knew how to use it, too! In minutes, we had taken care of the problem branch that I'd struggled with for an hour.

I hadn't asked her for help, but she had seen the need and freely given something that I'd never have thought to ask her for. Her soft-spoken personality just didn't shout, "I have a chainsaw!"

Sometimes people have hidden gifts. What is hanging on the wall in your garage? And could there be "chainsaw ladies" out there just waiting for the opportunity to share their unexpected gifts with you?

The Endless Circle

Savor this day and hold close the ones you love. Life is a gift.

C.S. Lewis pointed out that the people we meet in this life are the ones we will fellowship with forever in heaven. Eternity begins here. Today. It has to do with the immortal beings you eat lunch with and sit next to on the bus.

Celebrate the lives of those you love. Support their hopes and dreams. It only takes one person who will come into your life and say "You are important. You are beautiful." Pray for God's best in your life. If your heart and intention is to glorify God, He will bring you to people who will help you celebrate your life and who will stand with you.

When I talk to teens about dating and relationships,
I encourage them to look for another person with the
same faith. We all need big examples in our lives, people
who will gently push us towards the things of God and
also challenge our walk with Him.

> *Dear friends, we should love each other,*
> *because love comes from God. Everyone who*
> *loves has become God's child and knows*
> *God. . . . He sent his one and only Son into*
> *the world so that we could have life through*
> *him. . . . if God loved us that much we also*
> *should love each other. No one has ever seen*
> *God, but if we love each other, God lives in*
> *us, and his love is made perfect in us.*
>
> 1 JOHN 4:7, 9, 11, 12 NCV

Joining the Circle

I have received so many stories of God being faithful to His promises from others who have experienced loss. Their testimonies are amazing and remind me that believers form a circle of encouragement:

Soar Like Eagles

I had suddenly become a young widow, a single mom, and had moved to a new community. God's grace was sufficient as He planted us to make a difference in the lives of others who hurt. My life is blessed because of God's love to help work through the grief and to help others on this journey. Recently, I learned eagles don't fly around the storm; they fly through it, creating a vision of splendor when they arrive. We must go through the storm. God's love is sufficient to have a purpose as we endure the storms of life. We were meant to soar like the eagle.

~ *Elaine Cook*

Sunrise to Sunset

Just over a year ago I lost my youngest son to a tragic accident. He was 13 and the light and laughter of our lives. At first I was very angry at God for taking my son away from me. I felt that He had taken Garrett away, and I thought that I would never have joy or happiness in my life. Then things changed slowly and I realized that God had given me a way to be with my son again. By accepting Jesus Christ as my Lord and Savior, I will be reunited with Garrett as he had accepted Jesus as his Savior just one year before he died. I used to look at each passing day as another day without him. Now through my faith in God and His promise of eternal life, I thank Him for each sunrise and each sunset, because I know that it brings me one day closer to home with my God and Garrett.

LORI KELLY

Joining the Circle

Wise Instruction

When counseling people throughout his thirty-five years of ministry, my father was often asked, "Why am I having to go through this?" He would reply: "Would you rather God explain it to you or provide His grace and comfort during those tough times?" People would always answer something like this: "Good point, Pastor. It is not important that I fully understand why—just that I feel God's loving arms around me during this difficult time."

BETH MORTELL

Do not worry about anything,
but pray and ask God for everything you need,
always giving thanks. And God's peace,
which is so great we cannot understand it,
will keep your hearts and minds in Christ Jesus.
PHILIPPIANS 4:6, 7 NCV

"For I am persuaded
that neither death nor life,
nor angels nor principalities nor powers,
nor things present nor things to come,
nor height nor depth,
nor any other created thing,
shall be able to separate us
from the love of God
which is in Christ Jesus our Lord."

ROMANS 8:38-39 NKJV

ALL THE LORD'S WAYS ARE LOVING AND TRUE...
MY EYES ARE ALWAYS LOOKING
TO THE LORD FOR HELP.

PSALM 25:10, 15 NCV

You have not seen Christ,
but still you love him.
You cannot see him now,
but you believe in him.
So you are filled with a joy
that cannot be explained,
a joy full of glory.

1 PETER 1:8 NCV

Standing Tall

Without God I could have never made it when my world was turned upside down. My teenage son's life was football. On an October day, with only eight seconds left in the game, he was severely injured. His career, quality of life, and everything was gone! Today he lives in a wheelchair, paralyzed from the shoulders down. Yet his main focus is sharing his story and living God's plan. As he inspires others through his faith in God, his main goal is to stand tall beside his wheelchair. God's love is why I am able to live!

KEDDITH ANDREWS

The Spirit Himself bears witness with our spirit
that we are children of God, and if children,
then heirs—heirs of God and joint heirs with Christ,
if indeed we suffer with Him,
that we may also be glorified together.
ROMANS 8:16, 17 NKJV

For we walk by faith, not by sight . . .
We are confident . . .
>>*we make it our aim . . .*
>>*to be well pleasing to Him.*

2 CORINTHIANS 5:7–9 NKJV

>*For we know that if our earthly house, this tent,*
>>*is destroyed, we have a building from God,*
>*a house not made with hands, eternal in the heavens.*

2 CORINTHIANS 5:1 NKJV

We have small troubles for a while now,

but they are helping us gain an eternal glory

that is much greater than the troubles.

We set our eyes not on what we see

but on what we cannot see.

What we see will last only a short time,

but what we cannot see will last forever.

2 CORINTHIANS 4:17 NCV

Joining the Circle

Worship

Ten years ago I left a marriage that had devastated me emotionally, physically, spiritually, and financially. Things couldn't get any worse—until he committed suicide. I went from believing God would walk with me through the Valley of the Shadow of Death to knowing it for a fact, because He did so. Worship brought peace and hope. Through worship I could escape to His presence and experience His tender kindness in the midst of my pain.

Worship reminded me that He is deeper than my pain, bigger than any circumstance, and able to heal me. I could lose everything except eternal life with Jesus.

ANNI BARR

*[Jesus said] "He who believes in Me,
as the Scripture has said,
out of his heart will flow rivers of living water"*
JOHN 7:38 NKJV

Hope and Purpose

I just want people to know that God can take what's left of your life and give you a new purpose to continue on. When I heard these words from the doctor: "I'm sorry, there is nothing we can do," it cut to my heart with the force of an atomic bomb. My 11-year-old son, Dustin Tyler Brack, had lost control and hit a tree while snow skiing on our family vacation. In the blink of an eye nothing mattered to me—not a house, car, clothes, money… nothing!

Dustin wrote in his journal that he wanted "to minister to everyone," so I have committed my life to fulfilling his goal. When I get to heaven, I not only want to hear Jesus say, "Well done," but I want Dustin to run up to me and say, "Wow, Mom, you did an awesome job for me!" I thank God that He gave me this hope and purpose to keep going! He can do the same for you!

~ *Darla Brack*

Joining the Circle

A Gift of Love

It is in our greatest time of sorrow that our Heavenly Father is most near. My Savior was there when I was a pregnant teen living in a maternity home five hours away from my family and keeping my pregnancy a secret. Knowing from the beginning I needed to surrender my child up for adoption, I endured a very lonely time with the anticipation of a very difficult ending.

I delivered a beautiful, healthy baby boy. After three days together I walked down the hospital hall to hand him to the nurse. As I kissed his head and walked away I truly felt the "peace that passes all understanding" that can only come from the Holy Spirit.

After the sorrow, I have been blessed with a sweet husband and two precious children. God has allowed me after ten years to break free from the guilt and shame I had held for so long. It is through our greatest trials that His greatest strengths can be revealed to bring honor and glory to His name.

~ *Elizabeth Kilgore*

"PEACE I LEAVE WITH YOU,

MY PEACE I GIVE TO YOU;

NOT AS THE WORLD GIVES

DO I GIVE TO YOU.

LET NOT YOUR HEART BE TROUBLED,

NEITHER LET IT BE AFRAID."

JOHN 14:27 NKJV

Leaving Footprints

My husband, Trent, struggled to know what his purpose in life was. I sit on this side of heaven seeing that question fulfilled. The testimony of Trent's life still draws others to Christ when I share his story. I am able to minister to large groups of teens about our love story and how we surrendered our relationship to God. I talk to adults about how his dedication taught me to follow Christ. Trent's walk through this world is still marking a path for others to follow.

To live your life on earth in such a way that when you're gone it continues to impact others—even people whom you've never met—is the greatest purpose a believer can fulfill. Trent didn't think about that outcome as he humbly followed Jesus to the best of his ability—it was just a natural movement for him that ended up leaving a legacy here on earth.

Beloved, now we are children of God;
and it has not yet been revealed
    what we shall be,
but we know that when He is revealed,
    we shall be like Him,
for we shall see Him as He is.
And everyone who has this hope in Him
purifies himself,
    just as He is pure.

1 JOHN 3:2, 3 NKJV

WALK AS CHILDREN OF LIGHT

(FOR THE FRUIT OF THE SPIRIT IS IN ALL

GOODNESS, RIGHTEOUSNESS, AND TRUTH),

FINDING OUT WHAT IS ACCEPTABLE

TO THE LORD.

EPHESIANS 5:8, 9 NKJV

Trust with All Your Heart

One afternoon, I sat on a blanket reading some scripture verses and these simple thoughts came to mind again: "Tammy, choose life. Trust with all your heart and hold onto your Father in heaven."

This journey will never be easy. Maybe easier, but not easy. God's hand is still a mystery to me, and I probably would still trade in everything to have Trent back. Especially when I'm all alone and just want to grow old with the one I love. I wish I'd been able to tell him everything his life meant to me. I wish I had one more chance to tell him that I love him, that he changed my life, that he was the smartest man I ever knew. Just one more time to do something special for him and to see him smile.

My heart still belongs to Trent, and I keep my wedding ring on tight to honor him and all that I experienced through him. It's amazing how I can feel so complete inside living with a hole in my heart.

Many waters
cannot
quench love.

SONG OF SOLOMON 8:7 NKJV

Pace Yourself

All in all, I'm doing well and I can see the future clearly. It's hopeful, so I keep running this race. With my running shoes tied tightly, a bottle of water in my hand, and my sunglasses on, I pace myself. But there is a race ahead of me for the rest of my life.

DO YOU NOT KNOW THAT THOSE
WHO RUN IN A RACE ALL RUN,
BUT ONE RECEIVES THE PRIZE?
RUN IN SUCH A WAY THAT YOU MAY OBTAIN IT.
AND EVERYONE THAT COMPETES FOR THE PRIZE
IS TEMPERATE IN ALL THINGS.
NOW THEY DO IT TO OBTAIN A PERISHABLE CROWN;
BUT WE FOR AN IMPERISHABLE CROWN.
THEREFORE I RUN THUS: NOT WITH UNCERTAINLY.
THUS I FIGHT: NOT AS ONE THAT BEATS THE AIR.
BUT I DISCIPLINE MY BODY,
AND BRING IT INTO SUBJECTION, LEST,
WHEN I HAVE PREACHED TO OTHERS,
I MYSELF SHOULD BECOME DISQUALIFIED.

1 CORINTHIANS 9:24–27 NKJV

Physical running and exercising have been great therapy for me. I began to run and work out at a local YMCA as soon as I got settled back at home. I needed something to do during the quiet evenings when all the busyness of the day was over and the sun had set. If I sat alone in my house too long, I'd start to think about everything that had happened and create "what if" scenarios. My problems grew into mountains in my lonely thoughts, and I knew I couldn't let myself sink too far. I had to protect myself from sinking into grief past the point of no return.

Going to the gym every night created an atmosphere for me that I needed. Light and noise, without having to speak a word of my pain. Just me and God "working it out." And every once in a while "by chance" someone would come into the sauna and start talking about something I needed to hear at that very moment. It always made me laugh to know God would chase me down even in a sauna.

Let us run with patience the race that is set before us,
looking unto Jesus the author and finisher of our faith;
who for the joy that was set before him endured the cross,
despising the shame, and is set down
at the right hand of the throne of God.

HEBREWS 12:1 KJV

All Around You

Familiar scripture verses had surrounded my life for years, but in the difficult times each one took on a new meaning. Scripture immediately was a lifeline holding out hope. They wrapped me in comfort as I was desperately trying to figure out what went wrong and answer all the whys and find where God was in all of it. My relationship with His words changed to the extent that I understand them more and have applied them to my life more than ever before. I couldn't help but grow in the Lord as He put my life back together. Even though I don't care for the new plan, some days I even hate it, I do believe that I am walking in God's will for my life. I probably would change it in a heartbeat, but I also know I'm walking in my destiny now. I trust Him with my future. This is and was God's plan all along.

BUT HE KNOWS THE WAY THAT I TAKE;

WHEN HE HAS TESTED ME,

I SHALL COME FORTH AS GOLD.

JOB 23:10 NKJV

. . . It is painful, but later,
after we have learned from it,
we have peace . . .

HEBREWS 12:11 NCV

Looking Over Your Shoulder

I think I will always feel regrets. I don't feel regrets so much from teenage spats or splits, because I think those things just happen as we're maturing and trying to discover who we are as individuals, but I regret hurts in our marriage. Things I did. Things I said. Things I didn't say. Things I should have done. Trent was always my example, and I took that for granted. I sometimes find myself saying out loud before I go to bed, "I love you, Trent, and I'm so sorry I ever hurt you. Please forgive me. I wish you were here!"

If I didn't understand that God forgives, I couldn't let go of my regrets. I couldn't forgive myself. When I realize that all people are broken and with sin, but God fully forgives us, then I can forgive myself for all those shortcomings. I know that my husband understood that and would be the first to agree with God's perspective and forgive. We have to break the chain of unforgiveness by receiving God's promise of mercy.

If we say we have no sin,

we are fooling ourselves, and the truth is not in us.

But if we confess our sins, he will forgive our sins,

because we can trust God to do what is right.

He will cleanse us from all the wrongs we have done.

1 JOHN 1:8, 9 NCV

ALL HAVE SINNED AND ARE NOT
GOOD ENOUGH FOR GOD'S GLORY,
AND ALL NEED TO BE MADE RIGHT WITH GOD
BY HIS GRACE, WHICH IS A FREE GIFT.
THEY NEED TO BE MADE FREE FROM SIN
THROUGH JESUS CHRIST.
GOD GAVE HIM AS A WAY TO FORGIVE SIN
THROUGH FAITH IN THE BLOOD OF JESUS' DEATH.

ROMANS 3:23, 24 NCV

Take a Breath

My greatest healing came in taking a year off to allow the time to heal and to learn to rely on the Lord for everything. Not my music. Not my career. But God alone. I just simply let Him put my life back together again. I didn't know if I'd ever want to sing or write again. Honestly, I didn't want to. It took some time, but after a year, I walked back up on a platform and slowly began to sing and dance again. Yes, there has been great comfort and healing in that for me. There is joy in that for me again.

It's a new ministry now, and one I think my husband would be so proud of.

People who have heard my story have told me that they are inspired to keep following the Lord through their own struggles. They see a woman who seems to have every excuse to be depressed or to fall into bitterness, but there I am still singing and even laughing. I'm encouraging them as they see the faithful choices I've made after losing someone so close to me. They say, "There is someone who has gone before me into joy." And that testimony renews their strength. I want that peace to surround my life and draw others to Him.

". . . HE HAS SENT ME
TO HEAL THE BROKENHEARTED,
TO PROCLAIM LIBERTY
TO THE CAPTIVES . . ."
ISAIAH 61:1 NKJV

Steps of Healing

There is a lot of healing still going on in my life. I think I'll probably be healing the rest of my life from this. And even though I'm physically not married to Trent, he is still one of the biggest parts of my life. His example. His witness. His life. It is all a part of my deeper testimony now. My beloved is still in this with me, and I love that.

> "GOD IS LOVE.
> WHOEVER LIVES IN LOVE
> LIVES IN GOD,
> AND GOD IN HIM."
> 1 JOHN 4:16 NKJV

God's Word never fails to bring comfort. Many people have sent in testimonies like this one:

> There have been times in life when I felt I couldn't take another breath or face another day. The sorrow I felt was great; circumstances were hard. In these moments God's Word became hope for a better life. The Bible was His voice when I wasn't sure He cared. Life can be hard; we know it will be. When it is, we can hold on to His promises; they are certain. He never fails.
>
> He is near to the broken-hearted and He helps in times of trouble. He gives beauty for our ashes and joy for all the mourning.
>
> ~ *Deborah Bailey*

I am happy over your promises
as if I had found great treasure…
Those who love your teachings will find true peace,
and nothing will defeat them.

PSALM 119:162, 165 NCV

Sonshine

It's been raining for two days straight, but I somehow manage to find the warmth of the sun pushing
through the clouds. It's still the very thing that leads
me on…the sun…the Son!

God once said, "Let the light shine out of the darkness!"
This is the same God who made his light
shine in our hearts by letting us know
the glory of God that is in the face of Christ.
We have this treasure from God,
but we are like clay jars that hold the treasure.
This shows that the great power is from God,
not from us.
We have troubles all around us,
but we are not defeated.
We do not know what to do,
but we do not give up the hope of living.
We are persecuted,
but God does not leave us.
We are hurt sometimes,
but we are not destroyed.

2 CORINTHIANS 4:7–9 NCV

"These people who live in darkness
will see a great light.
They live in a place
covered with the shadows of death,
but a light will shine on them."

MATTHEW 4:16 NCV

HERE IS THE MESSAGE WE HAVE HEARD
FROM CHRIST AND NOW ANNOUNCE TO YOU:
GOD IS LIGHT AND IN HIM
THERE IS NO DARKNESS AT ALL.

1 JOHN 1:5 NCV

"You are the light that gives light to the world.
A city that is built on a hill cannot be hidden.
And people don't hide a light under a bowl.
They put it on a lampstand so the light shines
for all the people in the house. In the same way,
you should be a light for other people.
Live so that they will see the good things you do
and will praise your Father in heaven."

MATTHEW 5:14, 15 NCV

Easter Memories

During the church service a wave of memories flooded my mind as I remembered walking in and out of that very sanctuary with my husband many, many times before. It was our home church while growing up and growing into our marriage. I fought back the tears as I felt my lips whispering softly, "Where are you, Trent? I wish you were still here with me. I miss you so much and I hate being without you." Oh yes, there is still healing in my life as the clock spins around and around, but the longing and the memories and the deep love haven't faded even for one moment in my life. So I was glad to be there, in church on Easter Sunday celebrating the Resurrection of Jesus and Trent's new life.

Jesus said to him,
"I am the way, the truth, and the life.
No one comes to the Father except through Me.
If you had known Me, you would have known My Father also;
and from now on you know Him and have seen Him."

JOHN 14:6, 7 NKJV

"Let not your heart be troubled;
you believe in God, believe also in Me.
In My Father's house are many mansions;
if it were not so, I would have told you.
I go to prepare a place for you.
And if I go and prepare a place for you,
I will come again
and receive you to Myself;
that where I am,
there you may be also."

JOHN 14:1–3 NKJV

A Door to Forever

One Easter Sunday, I walked through the woods and began to walk up the pathway to Trent's grave. (It's so hard for me to say that word.) I sat down and stared off into the woods for probably five minutes until I couldn't hold back the tears anymore. I just cried and cried. And then I got up and started circling Trent's grave over and over again. Through my cries all I could say was, "Can you just get up, Trent! Can you just get up now!" Oh how I wished that could be reality. But I knew it wasn't, and I think that's why I couldn't stop crying. I finally pulled myself together. I thanked Jesus for the cross. I can't bring Trent back, but I will see him again. I will.

That is a promise because of that cross. Thank You, Jesus, for dying for Trent and me. Eternal life is so precious and truly a gift to all of us. What hope that brings! Even in the pains of life… there is hope. And with that thought, I got back into the car and headed down the road again.

It will never be easy for me. Never! But I was glad I went there on such a special day, Easter Sunday. I felt loved in that moment. In that place. How glorious it truly was. I can't help but feel a little closer to heaven each time I'm there. The presence of the Lord is always so strong… even in my pain…even in my tears. I am not alone.

"Jesus wept."
JOHN 11:35 NKJV

Cling to God

All our lives Trent and I had looked to God for guidance, for wisdom, for comfort. And so when I understood that my husband was gone from this world, even though my heart was breaking and I couldn't understand how God would allow such a thing to happen, I knew I didn't want to run away from Him. Desperate to cling to the only thing I knew was true, I found myself crying out to Him, "There are a million questions, and I don't understand any of this." As my body ached with sadness and confusion, I just kept asking God to remind me that He was real. And He did. Somehow, even though I didn't think I could ever endure such loss emotionally or physically, God let me know He was and is there. He is not a belief or a concept—He is my true Friend.

*Weeping may endure for a night,
but joy comes in the morning.*

PSALM 30:5 NKJV

To You I will cry, O LORD my Rock:

Do not be silent to me...

Blessed be the LORD because He has heard...

The LORD is my strength and my shield;

My heart trusted in Him, and I am helped;

Therefore my heart greatly rejoices,

and with my song I will praise Him...

Save Your people...

Shepherd them also,

And bear them up forever.

PSALM 28:1, 6, 7, 9 NKJV

He Understands Our Tears

What a beautiful fall day—the sky is blue and it's about 72 degrees outside. I'm sitting by the pool taking it all in. I have jeans and a sweater on, but at least my bare feet are getting a tan.

I take a deep breath as I listen to the gentle sounds of water rippling in the pool while the wind blows the trees in the woods behind me. I hear the birds playing and the leaves falling. It's so peaceful here. My heart is peaceful even through the tears that still fall.

YOU NUMBER MY WANDERINGS;

PUT MY TEARS INTO YOUR BOTTLE;

ARE THEY NOT IN YOUR BOOK?

PSALM 56:8 NKJV

put my tears into Your bottle

The Seasons of Memories

Fall is one of the hardest seasons for me. It will always remind me of leaving home with Trent to go to Jamaica in the late summertime and then coming back home without him in mid–October when autumn had arrived. So much had happened in my life during the season of change. The very smell of fall reminds me of the very first time I walked back into our home alone. How scared I was. How alone I felt. How confused I was. How my heart was shattered and broken. Despite all the hardships, I also remember how it felt good to be home. There was a feeling of peace in our home that was beyond understanding.

A special moment that I will always remember happened when I pushed the button to start our computer. I waited for the screen to light up, and then I caught my breath when I saw a little square appear in the lower left–hand corner. It looked like a sticky note stuck there on the screen. It said, "Tammy is who I dream of. Can't wait to see you."

I sat there, stunned, by the message Trent had left for me to find. I was amazed how he continued to comfort me, even from heaven.

Keep on loving each other.

HEBREWS 13:1 NCV

We're In This Together

Even though it's still so hard for me, I'm reminded today of God's love for me. His healing touch. The way He provides. How understanding He is. How He's honestly taken care of me. Now, that doesn't mean I'm all healed and on the other side. Quite the contrary. I think I'll be healing the rest of my life, and most days I still feel like I'm only halfway there. But I'm moving forward and trusting in the Lord, even though I don't always understand. He's right there with me.

> Those who sat in darkness and in the shadow of death,
> Bound in affliction and irons . . .
> They fell down, and there was none to help.
> Then they cried out to the LORD in their trouble,
> And He saved them out of their distresses.
> He brought them out of the darkness
> and the shadow of death,
> And broke their chains in pieces.
>
> PSALM 107:10, 12–14 NKJV

Why am I so sad?

Why am I so upset?

I should put my hope in God,

And keep praising him,

my Savior and my God.

PSALM 42:11 NCV

He Feels Our Pain

I had a vision not that long ago. I was driving home from a friend's house, and I couldn't stop crying. I looked over at the passenger's side and could almost see Jesus. He reached out for my hand, said nothing, and with the sweetest loving look on His face, He just cried with me. I remember that vision whenever I can't stop crying. What comfort to know He hurts when we hurt.

SINCE WE HAVE A GREAT HIGH PRIEST,

JESUS THE SON OF GOD,

WHO HAS GONE INTO HEAVEN,

LET US HOLD ON TO THE FAITH WE HAVE.

FOR OUR HIGH PRIEST IS ABLE

TO UNDERSTAND OUR WEAKNESSES.

WHEN HE LIVED ON EARTH

HE WAS TEMPTED IN EVERY WAY THAT WE ARE,

BUT HE DID NOT SIN.

LET US FEEL VERY SURE

THAT WE CAN COME BEFORE GOD'S THRONE

WHERE THERE IS GRACE.

THERE WE CAN RECEIVE MERCY

AND GRACE TO HELP US

WHEN WE NEED IT.

HEBREWS 4:14–16 NCV

That Long Walk

The walk along the half-mile trail to where Trent is buried will always be filled with the most painful steps I will ever have to take. The deepest sorrow and grief came over me one of those times, and I felt as if I couldn't take another step. This is where my friends' prayers reached me and gave me strength outside of my own, because somehow I took another step and another until making it through the woods to the top of that hill. It was a beautiful afternoon as I watched just one butterfly playing around me. I sat in the chair, put on my headphones, and listened to my song "Father God" repeatedly as I held my Bible in my arms. With tears falling from my eyes, I felt the peace of God and slowly fell asleep right there. I could have stayed there all day.

Isn't it funny? I don't like going there, but once I get there I have a hard time leaving. After about three hours, I sat up, placed my *Breathing* CD on the ground next to Trent (as if to leave one for him) and kissed the memorial cross that stands before him.

I look to the hills, but where does my help come from?

My help comes from the LORD, who made heaven and earth.

He will not let you be defeated.

He who guards you never sleeps....

The LORD is the shade that protects you from the sun.

The sun cannot hurt you during the day,

and the moon cannot hurt you at night.

The LORD will protect you from all dangers;

he will guard your life.

The LORD will guard you as you come and go,

both now and forever.

PSALM 121 NCV

God's Treasure-Hunter

The walk back to my car from Trent's gravesite gets easier with time, and God continually reminds me that He is with me. Once I spotted a yellow snake under a fallen tree. You might not think that would be an encouraging sign, but it was for me because Trent loved snakes. He even had a fifteen-foot python that he would take to children's schools for show-and-tell. And his favorite color was yellow. Because Trent was colorblind, that was the one color he could see clearly. I got a smile on my face at that moment. I hate snakes (and this one was staring at me) but it was another reminder from God that I am not alone. He's always thinking about me.

If you don't stop and look, you'll miss God's reminders. But if you seek, you will find that all your treasures are being stored up in heaven. Here, we're all just passing through. I got to experience one of my heavenly treasures early. His name is Trent Lenderink.

"DON'T STORE TREASURES FOR YOURSELVES HERE
ON EARTH WHERE MOTHS AND RUST WILL DESTROY
THEM AND THIEVES CAN BREAK IN AND STEAL THEM.
BUT STORE YOUR TREASURES IN HEAVEN
WHERE THEY CANNOT BE DESTROYED BY MOTHS
OR RUST AND WHERE THIEVES CANNOT BREAK IN
AND STEAL THEM. YOUR HEART WILL BE
WHERE YOUR TREASURE IS."

MATTHEW 6:21 NCV

"The kingdom of heaven
is like a treasure hidden in a field.
One day a man found the treasure
and then he hid it in the field again.
He was so happy that he went
and sold everything he owned to buy that field.
Also, the kingdom of heaven is like a man
looking for fine pearls.
When he found a very valuable pearl,
he went and sold everything he had
and bought it."

MATTHEW 13:44, 45 NCV

Familiar Steps

If you really believe with your whole heart that God is in control of your life, then you'll trust Him with it no matter what. We all imagine what life might be like if circumstances were different—but we live in the reality of the life that has been given us.

A woman sent me an email of how she was praying for me because God had shown her that I sometimes pictured my husband coming back through the door into our home. That was true. I did. Seeing Trent come through the door was just such a familiar sight. I sometimes look at that door and can still see him opening it.

you really believe that God is in control of your life with

n you'll trust Him with it no matter what.

all imagine what life might be like if circumstances were different—

t we live in the reality of the life that has been given us.

But what do I do with that? At first I just fell to the ground and cried out to God. I had to mourn the loss of that moment. I sit here on this couch now, three years later, looking at that door. Somehow, God is enough. I'm choosing joy. One day at a time with the Lord, every day.

I think we all can picture someone coming in the door who could change our circumstances. But the reality is that Trent isn't coming home. The situation isn't going to change. This is my life now. But although I can't change this, I can change the out-come with the help of God. This is my part of the story. I get to write the next chapter by what I do with this life I have now. The choices I make become the words to the next chapters.

Look Around

Look for God. Look for Him in your circumstance. He is there. If you challenge yourself to look for Him, you will find Him near.

At the beginning of your loss, the situation is all about you: your loss, your situation, your feelings. You need time to process that. Then you look beyond the sorrow and cry out, "Where are You, Jesus?" That is when you realize that you are not alone. Then you are able to say with certainty that God is enough.

I think you first have to be allowed to process those inner feelings that are more about you. If people or circumstances push you to skip over that seemingly selfish part, you will have to deal with it later. You'll have to backtrack and work through that stage. You can't ignore what has happened to you as an individual. Your life has changed, and it doesn't seem like anything good can come of that. I was allowed to go through that process of mourning, and I think that's why, years later, I can stand here and say God is healing me and that I've come through to the other side of sorrow.

Individual Styles

Someone sent me a poem that says grief is as individual as a fingerprint. We all have our own ways of dealing with this visitor—our constant companion after a loss. But we learn so much about ourselves, about our lives, from it. Like a mirror we see ourselves in its reflection, and we see that we are capable of strength, love, goodness, and humility. We see the love of our family and friends and the love of God being poured into our lives. We realize that we are vessels to both give and receive blessing. Before our sorrow, we may have been blessed to give. After, we learn the blessing of receiving.

My best friend, Pam Thum, and her husband,
Steve, gave me this letter a year after my loss:

Dear Tammy,

We're celebrating a covenant with you

that goes way beyond this world. It wraps

around the farthest star, bounces off the top

of the universe, and kisses the heart of a boy

in the next world. I believe it started

one day but never stops for eternity!

A big hug and kiss from us to you in

celebrating love…the forever kind.

Steve & Pam

Leading Others Through Their Sorrow

You can give precious gifts to people you care about when they are grieving. Most of them involve just saying "That's okay, I'm here for you" without further comment!

1. Allow them time to grieve. Give them permission to pause. Grief pulls the rug out from under us, and we need to sit a minute to get our bearings before we try to stand.

2. Give them permission to confess. We deal with disappointment in every part of our being, including our fleshly nature. Sometimes we need to confess that we are "unspiritual" in our reaction to grief. I had friends who were patient and non-judging when I cried out, "I hate this!"

3. Give them permission to be angry. God can take our anger. He knows we might be angry with Him, even when He is trying to heal us. He waits patiently, like a rock in the storm of our emotion, for us to turn and receive His help.

4. Give them permission to move on when they are ready. Sometimes a person who is coming out on the other side of grief almost feels apologetic for moving beyond sorrow into a new life. Let them know this is okay.

5. Help them give the future, as well as the past, to Jesus. "What ifs" apply to both the past and the future. Share support from prayer, scripture, and personal experience about trusting God.

6. Celebrate with them as positive emotions return. Laugh. Be silly together. Remind them that you care about them just as much in the lighthearted times as in sorrow.

Share the Joy

Being happy in others' triumph helps us learn to find happiness in ourselves. I was so thrilled to read this testimony that a reader sent. She didn't give up!

About two years ago, my boyfriend of over four years broke off our relationship. As anyone can imagine, I was crushed and heartbroken. This was the man who I was supposed to marry. We had the ring picked out and was it ever beautiful! After the breakup, I became hurt and was very angry at God. I kept asking, "Why is God doing this to me?"

About eight months later, I hit rock bottom. I turned away from my family and God. I was so angry with Him. After all, He was ruining my plans for my life. Once I hit rock bottom, I realized I couldn't do this anymore on my own. I had to turn back to God and ask Him for help. I do know God was there all along. He was just standing back waiting for me to turn back around to Him. He brought me back out of my depression and helped me to realize that there was hope that life would go on, even though I thought my life couldn't get any worse. My advice to any girl who is going through a breakup or divorce: turn to God as soon as you can. It's not worth the heartache and pain that you put yourself through without the help of your Heavenly Father showing you that there is light. Although it may be dim at first, it will get brighter over time.

JULIE WILLIAMS

In the Arms of Family

I am blessed to spend time with my family. My
favorite place to be. In the arms of my family. Always
love. Always joy. Always adventure. Always there.

My mom shared these thoughts about my loss in my book *Learning to Breathe Again*:

> When I think back on that experience, as difficult as it was, I'm amazed by how God sends His grace in the most painful and frightening situations. In the hours following Tammy's call with the news that Trent was missing, peace filled my mind as I thought of the healing that had occurred just weeks earlier between Tammy's dad and me. Trent's passion for life and love was responsible.... Walls came down that night, and we laughed and enjoyed our time together.... I felt a great warmth, understanding then that forgiveness is the best medicine in the world.... the Holy Spirit reminded me of Jesus' promise to Tammy—to all of us: "I will never leave you or forsake you." And, "I will send you a comforter."

. . . He Himself has said, "I will never leave you
nor forsake you."
So we may boldly say:
"The LORD is my helper; I will not fear."
HEBREWS 13:5, 6 NKJV

He Will Carry You

God's Word was my strength immediately after I lost
my husband and continues to be my source of comfort
today. One of the Psalms that helped me in the first
days of my sorrow was Psalm 30. I opened my Bible
and immediately my eye fell on the fifth verse. This is
how I read that passage:

*Although you may mourn throughout the night
and sorrow will endure throughout the night—
probably throughout many nights, Tammy—
My joy will always come in the morning. My joy
will always meet you in the morning. When you
feel like you can't breathe, when you feel like you
can't walk, when you can't see, when you can't
get through the day…I'm still there carrying
you. When you can't breathe one more time,
then just rest your head on the pillow, and I'll
be right there beside you. When you wake up
the next morning, I'll be right there beside you.
My joy will cover you. And joy will be the
very thing that will bring you back to life again,
because without it, you'll never survive this grief.
Just trust Me, Tammy. Trust Me.*

Let It Go

WORDS & MUSIC BY TAMMY TRENT

No matter where you go
Or where you're from,
He watches over you from above.
He looks inside your heart
And sees your face.
Whenever there is pain,
He brings His grace.
So, let it go and be free.
Let it go and you'll see.
Jesus can heal anything
If you believe.
Let it go.
No matter how you feel,
You're not alone.
He's standing by your side
To lead you home.
With all that you've been through,
You must press on.
I know that He would want you
To be strong.

[JESUS SAID,] "COME TO ME,

ALL YOU WHO LABOR AND ARE HEAVY LADEN,

AND I WILL GIVE YOU REST.

TAKE MY YOKE UPON YOU AND LEARN FROM ME,

FOR I AM GENTLE AND LOWLY IN HEART,

AND YOU WILL FIND REST FOR YOUR SOULS.

FOR MY YOKE IS EASY

AND MY BURDEN IS LIGHT."

MATTHEW 11:28–30 NKJV

Uplifting Notes

Sometimes the Lord shows me His encouragement through the words of others. Close friends, or sometimes even strangers, send notes of encouragement just when I need them most. Here is one from my close friend Pete Orta that is such a beautiful word–picture of what he saw happening in my life:

...d to live out that belief in God's plan when tragedy st...

...d had been part of my life since I was a child,

...t sometimes it seemed like I was praying to someone wh...

...t sitting next to me on my couch. But His presence has...

...ce I lost Trent. I had to just depend on Him in a close...

...d He has met me there. He has kept His promise to go...

...ough the dark days, comfort me with His love, and lea...

Dear Tammy,

You are like an iron glove with a glass fist inside. Life has come at you head on, and you are standing strong. Even if your legs give out on you sometimes, your spirit keeps running. You have the softest insides, because your outside has had to be so tough. It has protected your heart and your dreams. Now life has been able to touch your heart, and it hurts even more than most people's. Hurt has walked in and it won't leave like you want it to. But I sit back and watch your spirit inside get a little stronger and the outside get a little softer. You will be able to explain life by not being able to explain life. You will be able to understand life because you are not able to understand life. Knowledge in life is experience; it's not being able to explain everything. It's like a blind person will only stumble in a room where they have never been. You have had to walk through a cold dark room, and the knowledge of that will set people free. There's not an answer in words; there's only knowledge in your experience. And with that experience you will change the world!

There is a future in your life. I'm just sorry you were not able to choose it.

Love,
Pete

Uplifting Notes

Dear Tammy,

My husband, age 27, passed away in November. The Lord showed me that I needed to allow Him to come in and fill this endless gap. As I did, the pain was intensified because this sorrowful room was illuminated. I then received this phrase:

To feel + to deal = to HEAL.

As I allowed Him to enter this painful place, it did illuminate the vastness of its size, but I would continue to not resist the pain. He would reveal issues and memories that hurt, but I accepted them, dealt with it, and gave it back to Him as He brought healing to my heart.

CARI STEWART

Dear Tammy,

I, too, fell madly in love with my teenage sweetheart! We married while still in high school. At 44, he died in an accident. No chance to say "Goodbye", "I'm sorry", "I love you"…the usual things you wish you could say just one last time.

So many regrets, so many questions: "Why? Why now, after struggling to get by, raise a family…?" This was supposed to be "our time"—time to be together, grow old together…but now he was gone. I felt my heart would burst; many times I wished it would. You see, over the years, Jesus had knocked at my heart's door, but I wouldn't let Him in. Then, when nothing could ease the ache or fill the void in my heart, He knocked again. My Savior forgave me. He lifted me up and gave me such peace and joy. He showed me that I could still live…laugh…love again, and that as a child of God, I am worthy to be loved! I remarried seven years ago. Mike's love for Christ carries over into every aspect of his life and our marriage. When I look at him, I see Jesus and I have to say, "Thank you, Lord! I wouldn't change a thing!"

Wanda Jessup

Gifted

People say how I've inspired them, but honestly, I'm inspired by their love and prayers and support for me. Especially when I'm a girl they don't even know. In some letters people just open up their hearts to me as if we have been friends for years. Love is an amazing gift.

Dear Tammy,

It's hard opening doors inside yourself to places you vowed never to go. Never revisiting the pain because it reminds you that life is not perfect. Never recalling the loneliness because it reminds you that you are not self-sufficient. Yet when I revisit those places of trial, I can see how the hand of God was there even though I could not see it. The times in my life where I felt the weakest, the times when I thought I could not run this race of life one more mile, those were the times God made me strong.

~ *Jenn Bodnar*

Dear Tammy,

When I was 22 and single, I found out that I was pregnant. I thought my world was coming to an end. But my mom told me something that completely changed me. She told me I had to let the Lord give me joy in the situation. That one sentence completely changed how I felt about my situation. When I allowed the Lord to give me joy I found that things were not as bad as I thought they were. I realized that God loved me no matter what and it didn't matter what other people thought or said about me.

That was nearly fourteen years ago, and now I have a son who wants to be a youth pastor when he grows up. So, no matter what things look like, let God give you joy and you really will make it through no matter how bad things seem. God Bless!

AMORETTE HELM

Patterns of Promise

From generation to generation, God has revealed Himself as a personal God who wants an intimate relationship with each one of us. He wants us to know Him, talk to Him, and trust Him.

God promises to help us in difficult times. "Do not be afraid or discouraged, for the LORD is the one who goes before you. He will be with you; He will neither fail you nor forsake you" (DEUTERONOMY 31:8 NLT). When pain and suffering strike and doubts flood your mind, put your confidence in the living God. He will never let you down.

We'll never be able to find an explanation for all circumstances in life, but we must remember that God is in control. The Bible says that God's thoughts are not our thoughts and His ways are not our ways (ISAIAH 55:8). God is sovereign and nothing in our life escapes Him. "God has made everything beautiful for its own time. He has planted eternity in the human heart, but even so, people cannot see the whole scope of God's work from beginning to end" (ECCLESIASTES 3:11 NLT).

Instead of asking God "why" about the pain, ask "what next" and "how."

STEVE RUSSO

Father & Daughter Dance

I always wondered why I was different. Growing up I knew my friends had something I did not. It bothered me some, but for the most part I never asked any questions. Then one day while sitting with my mom, those difficult words escaped my mouth: "Why do I not have a dad?"

My mother explained that upon conceiving me out of wedlock, my father did not want anyone to know I was his child and instantly left my mother's life. From that moment, the most heartbreaking revelation became planted in my mind: "I was not wanted!" I've struggled many times with that thought, but God's love and grace have always given me a hope that draws me closer to Him. God has encouraged me that although I have never known an earthly father, He is my one true Father! In His own words God reminds me of that each time I read Psalm 68:5, "[God is] a father to the fatherless."

Leigh Ellen Eades

He is a father to orphans,

and he defends widows.

God gives the lonely a home.

He leads prisoners out with joy…

Praise the Lord, God our Savior,

who helps us every day.

Our God is a God who saves us;

the LORD God saves us from death…

God, people have seen your victory march;

God my King marched into the holy place.

The singers are in front

and the instruments are behind.

In the middle are the girls with the tambourines.

Praise God in the meeting place.

PSALM 68:5, 6, 19, 20, 24–26 NCV

Hidden Treasure

At the age of 47, I was lying in bed in the hospital prepared for a lumpectomy. I had taken my Bible with me and was reading it when my eyes fell on the passage "Man shall take a weapon to you and it shall do you no harm." I closed my Bible, was totally confident that there was no cancer. I was going to be fine. My surgeon came in that evening before surgery, asked if I was okay and if my husband would be there with me the next morning during surgery. I replied that I told him to go to work, as we needed the money for our expenses and we were both confident God had spoken. I shared the passage from the Bible with the surgeon who replied that he was a Christian, also.

No cancer was found during the surgery. Later, I searched the Bible over trying to find that comforting passage again, but was unsuccessful. One day, I saw a preacher on TV offering an engraved coin that you carry in your pocket. The passage of Scripture imprinted on it was Isaiah 54:17, "Man shall take a weapon to you and it shall do you no harm." I sent for two of them! To this day my husband and I carry those coins as a reminder of the grace and love of God and how He gave me confidence at a very troubling time.

MAXINE LEATHLEY

Whatever It Takes, Lord

My story of hope and grace does not compare to Tammy losing her sweetheart, but for moms who have an unsaved child I give you this: God loves him or her more than you do. I was at the point of breaking down until God reminded me that, as it is with everything else in this life, I never owned my son. I was only borrowing Bobby from the Lord as Samuel's mother did when he was growing up. I found hope in knowing that God's grace is sufficient and He has a plan for Bobby that I could never fulfill. His love is greater than anything I could ever conceive.

I laid on my face before the Lord one night and said, "Thy will be done in his life." I asked God to release me of any guilt I felt, to give me the strength to watch Bobby's trials, and to allow me to help another mom one day. As I sat in a courtroom to hear my son be given ten months in a federal prison, the words "Thy will be done" rose inside of me, and a peace washed over me that can only come from God. Though there was pain, the peace was strong. So I say: rest in God's peace and continue to walk in the anointing He has placed on your life that the world may see His grace.

Kimberly H. Byrum

Grace Full

My life's passion is to rest in God's hope. The hope I have comes from a deep assurance that God promises to transform ashes into beauty. I have dwarfism, and sometimes it feels hopeless to overcome the stereotypes others have of me. Etched in our minds and hearts are statements we have been labeled with.

The One with all authority to label or condemn does not do so. With Christ, every label was nailed to the cross. We now live in God's promises of a new identity. What hope! Slough off limiting labels and begin to view yourself the way Christ does.

JEN MONTZINGO

…give them beauty for ashes,

The oil of joy for mourning,

The garment of praise for the spirit of heaviness;

that they may be called trees of righteousness,

the planting of the LORD, that He may be glorified….

Instead of your shame you shall have double honor,

and instead of confusion they shall rejoice in their portion.

Therefore in their land they shall possess double;

Everlasting joy shall be theirs….

"All who see them shall acknowledge them,

That they are the posterity whom the LORD has blessed."

ISAIAH 61:3, 7, 9 NKJV

Dance of Healing

At our family Christmas celebration five years ago, my sister and I had a huge fight that caused us not to speak to each other for more than a year. The rift between us was so insurmountable that my sister did not come to my wedding when I got married in January of the next year. At the time of our fight, I had just returned to a close walk with the Lord. My sister was in a bad marriage and was not walking with God. However, five years later my sister is remarried to an awesome godly man, I am married to an awesome godly man, and our relationship, with Christ at the center, could not be better.

A year ago my sister moved from Oklahoma to Florida and I was devastated for her to be so far away. However, both of us were trusting God's direction for her life. Even when there seems to be no hope in a situation, Christ can bring healing of hearts and healing of lives.

M. VOLREL

God has chosen you and made you his holy people.

He loves you. So always do these things:

Show mercy to others, be kind,

humble, gentle, and patient.

Get along with each other, and forgive each other.

If someone does wrong to you,

forgive that person because the Lord forgave you.

Do all these things;

but most important, love each other.

Love is what holds you all together in perfect unity.

Let the peace that Christ gives control your thinking,

because you are all called together

in one body to have peace.

Always be thankful.

Let the teaching of Christ live in you richly.

COLOSSIANS 3:12–16 NCV

Hold On

The only pain worse than the abuse one receives at the hand of another, is the pain that's self–induced, that comes from low self–worth, lack of focus, ambition, and fear. The enemy likes nothing more than for us to be so consumed with what we've done that we forget Whose we are. At your lowest times—times when you feel that there's no turning back from the mistakes you have made—hold on to the fact that with every breath, therein lies a new opportunity to grow, to change, to discover God's purpose for your life. Trust me, it's bigger than anything you've already done—good or bad.

SHELLIE R. WARREN

I ask the Father in his great glory
to give you the power to be strong inwardly
through his Spirit. I pray that Christ will live
in your hearts by faith and that your life
will be strong in love and be built on love.
And I pray that you and all God's holy people
will have the power to understand
the greatness of Christ's love—
how wide and how long and how deep
that love is. Christ's love is greater
than anyone can ever know, but I pray
that you will be able to know that love.
Then you can be filled with the fullness of God.
With God's power working in us,
God can do much, much more than
anything we can ask or imagine.

EPHESIANS 3:16–20 NCV

Warrior's Dance

My story of hope is one of survival. My childhood memories are of seeing my parents suffer with diseases. My mother was diagnosed with cancer when I was 12, and she was not expected to live five years. At the same time, my father was dealing with rheumatoid arthritis. For eleven years he had one surgery a year.

I was fearful of my parents abandoning me by death. As a teenager, I sank into depression and thought of suicide daily, though I attended church often.

My dad died when I was 19. He thought he was going to faint, started to fall, and I caught him. We both fell to the floor, and he died right there. I watched his life disappear. My mother passed away seven years later, the

day after I returned from my honeymoon. It wasn't until my child reached three years old that I sank into depression over losing my parents.

A friend gave me a book called *This Present Darkness* by Frank Peretti that truly opened my eyes to spiritual warfare. I discovered how to fight for my life, my heart, my emotions, and my mind through prayer. Satan longs to use our past to hold us down through self-pity, guilt, loneliness, and feelings of abandonment.

Even though losing my parents hurt me deeply, it's given me a platform to talk to youth about respecting and loving their parents. When you tell a story of brokenness and can paint a picture of reality to our youth, they listen. I now have fully embraced hope that I will see my parents again, face-to-face. It's taught me to really live each day to the fullest, love my kids more, and have compassion for the weary.

~ *Lisa Bevill*

Testing

It has been said, "Out of the test, the testimony comes." I say, "out of our mess, our ministry was birthed." In the past couple of years, our ministry and family suffered many attacks and difficult circumstances that threatened to derail our very existence. My faith was not only tested, but it seemed broken beyond repair as I witnessed the enemy's attempts to destroy my beautiful daughters. We experienced betrayal, rejection, abuse, sickness, and despair. But the foundation of faith was strong. What the enemy meant for harm, God has turned into a harmony of powerful testimonies. Jeremiah 29:11 has been our hope, "I know the plans I have for you says the LORD, plans to prosper you, to give you hope and a future." Our motto is: Faith is stepping out on nothing and feeling it become something.

JENNIFER J PASQUALE

He who dwells in the secret place
of the Most High
Shall abide under the shadow of the Almighty.
I will say of the LORD,
"He is my refuge and my fortress,
My God, in Him I will trust."
Surely He shall deliver you from
the snare of the fowler
And from the perilous pestilence.
He shall cover you with His feathers,
And under His wings you shall take refuge;
His truth shall be your shield and buckler.
You shall not be afraid of the terror by night . . .
For he shall give His angels charge over you
To keep you in all your ways.

PSALM 91:1–5, 11 NKJV

Arms of the Savior

I choose joy! Inner joy. My beloved husband of twenty-five years passed away five months ago, suddenly, without warning. That inner joy I speak of is the steady assurance of God's presence in my life. He knows my future and I am in His hands. There are and will be very hard times. I know I will not "get over it," but with God's grace I will "get through it."

Oh, I still hurt, cry, grieve, and wonder why my beloved was taken so early. But I also have an inner peace and joy that reigns in my life. An assurance that Bart is in the strong and capable arms of our Savior, and so am I... here on earth for a little while longer.

COLETTE MEREDITH

I will praise You with my whole heart;

…And praise Your name

For Your loving kindness and Your truth;

For You have magnified Your word

above all Your name.

In the day when I cried out, You answered me,

And made me bold with strength in my soul….

Though I walk in the midst of trouble,

You will revive me;

…And Your right hand will save me.

The LORD will perfect that which concerns me;

Your mercy, O LORD, endures forever;

Do not forsake the works of Your hands.

PSALM 138:1–3, 7, 8 NKJV

Night of Tears

A phone call from a police officer late at night and my seemingly idyllic life blew up in my face. My seventeen-year marriage to my pastor husband was over. In that one moment everything changed. I found myself alone in the city of Houston, Texas, after moving here only six months before. I had no family here and had two little girls, ages 12 and 9, depending on me. It was time for me to depend on the promise that God had made, "I will never leave you or forsake you." And He never has. My favorite prayer throughout the process of getting on with this new life was: "God, don't let a bitter woman raise my children, even if the bitter woman is me!" He has answered that prayer!

I am able to see my life with such joy...the befores and the afters! I even travel the country ministering with stand-up comedy to offer that kind of "joy after sorrow" to others. I have lived in the night of tears...but most of my life has moved forward into the beautiful joy that cometh in the morning! If I am to choose... I choose JOY!

SUSAN O'DONNELL

"... THE LORD, IS MY STRENGTH AND SONG;

HE ALSO HAS BECOME MY SALVATION."

THEREFORE WITH JOY YOU WILL DRAW WATER

FROM THE WELLS OF SALVATION.

AND IN THAT DAY YOU WILL SAY:

"PRAISE THE LORD, CALL UPON HIS NAME;

DECLARE HIS DEEDS AMONG THE PEOPLES,

... SING TO THE LORD,

FOR HE HAS DONE EXCELLENT THINGS."

ISAIAH 12:2–5 NKJV

Timing Things

I can recall visiting my grandmother at her home near the ocean. I was privately going through some rough times. Somehow she knew. As we both sat on the bench facing the Atlantic Ocean, she turned to me and said, "Troubles are like the waves of the ocean: they will come, but they have to go." It brought back to me the scripture in Ecclesiastes that speaks of times for everything. She was right; my times of trouble come and go, but the sun still shines and the beach still stands…and so do I.

THOM ROBERTS

To everything there is a season,
A time for every purpose under heaven:
A time to be born,
And a time to die;
A time to plant,
And a time to pluck what is planted;
A time to kill,
And a time to heal,
A time to break down,
And a time to build up,
A time to weep,
And a time to laugh;
A time to mourn,
And a time to dance;
…He has made everything beautiful in its time.

ECCLESIASTES 3:1–4, 11 NKJV

Standing Close

People often ask me what they can do for friends who are experiencing loss. I responded to a pastor this way: I think the biggest role you can play is being there if and when they need you. Just you. Not even your words necessarily, but your love and prayers. Standing in the gap for them when they cannot stand alone... when they don't know what to pray. In the days to come, find people to bring meals...to send cards...to mow the grass...to clean the house...to run errands. People in sorrow may not ask for help, but they will love knowing they are not facing this loss alone. Give them space if they need it... time...few words are better because there are no fitting words in these moments. We know Jesus is our comforter, but allow others to find that for themselves, too. Stay close in case they need you to pick them up emotionally or spiritually.

You can be God's love letter to those who need Him.

YOU YOURSELVES ARE OUR LETTER,

WRITTEN ON OUR HEARTS,

KNOWN AND READ BY EVERYONE.

YOU SHOW THAT YOU ARE A LETTER FROM CHRIST...

NOT WRITTEN WITH INK

BUT WITH THE SPIRIT OF THE LIVING GOD.

IT IS NOT WRITTEN ON STONE TABLETS

BUT ON HUMAN HEARTS.

2 CORINTHIANS 3:2–4 NCV

Taking Steps

One bit of wisdom that I learned from my experience of loss was that I needed to take care of myself. I actually had to look at myself from the outside and remember to do things for my mental and spiritual health. It's true that there are ways to be an encouragement to yourself! Here are some ideas that helped me:

- Play music that encourages you. A song can contain a message that we "get" more than a sermon. Have ready a selection of CDs that inspire you or make you dance. Play them in your home and car. Jog or exercise to music. Sing your prayers.

- Exercise regularly. Everyone has their own idea of what "good exercise" is, but we can all do something to maintain our health and encourage a healthy outlook. Walk, stretch, dance in front of the mirror, go on a bike ride, swim laps, or work in the yard.

- Post scripture promises and encouraging words and notes from friends around your home, car, and workplace. I hung a decorative sign over my office door that reads: "Breathe!" A sign in my kitchen says, "Believe!" I still have the "sticky" note that Trent left on our computer that says "Can't Wait to See You!"

- Plan a trip. Give yourself something to look forward to. Go back to places that were special to you as a child, and visit friends and family who will support your growth on this journey.

- Get a massage when you can. For the first year after I lost Trent, every Tuesday at 10 p.m., I was given a massage at my home by a sweet Christian girl named Rondolyn Florence, who felt she was supposed to give to me. There is healing in touch. There is healing in releasing what's deep inside. A massage can be a safe and peaceful place to let go and let God.

Goals

I set realistic goals for each day. I may have an impossible list of things that need taking care of, but I prioritize things that are most important and possible to get done in one day. For the leftover things—there's always tomorrow!

In setting goals for myself and my growth beyond the sorrow, I realize I will never be perfect. But there needs to be progress. Small triumphs, like getting my closet organized, show me that I'm moving forward. Letting go a little bit at a time brings healing.

I journal my needs, as well as God's answers to prayer. Looking back over prayer requests that have been answered helps me realize I am progressing. Re–reading my hopes and goals often helps me keep focused on the future.

Use creative techniques along with journaling. I once drew a cross, cut it out, and then wrote out my frustrations, anger, and pain on it. Then I stood over a trash can and ripped it up and threw it away. "I'm letting go! It is finished!" I shouted, remembering Jesus' sacrifice on the cross.

Find a Bible devotional that you can understand. Don't give up. Keep looking for one that works for you to use every day. Fight for your spiritual life!

Reach Out

Hold up your testimony for other people's sake. I have lost count of how many times people have told me, "I was ready to give up because my trials were so hard, but when I heard your story, I said 'If Tammy can go through all that, I can make it through my troubles.'"

We have all suffered in this world to some degree. Those of us who have experienced deep loss need the comfort of others who have gone before us. Somehow that makes the fight a little easier. We all have a place where our testimony is a light in the darkness to those who need to hear a word of encouragement or see a person who is standing strong in the face of difficulty. Even if they are not in need of your advice today, people will remember your story when they face trials in the future.

Remember that young people are watching. You are a mentor and one who holds up a standard against the darkness of this world in which they live. How can your testimony change the world around you for God? Your home? Your school? Your workplace? It only takes a small candle to light up a whole room that is in darkness. You don't have to have a great singing voice or eloquent speech to say a few encouraging words that will open up someone's heart to healing. Sometimes no words are necessary—a smile or a gentle hand on someone's shoulder is all that is needed to turn their day around, or better yet, turn around their life!

Memories

Surround yourself with memories. Cherish the old ones and remember to create new ones. I have our wedding portrait on the wall surrounded by three ceramic crosses with the words *believe, hope,* and *faith* engraved on them. I have photos of us together all around the house just as they've always been. I don't want to forget the hope that I have in Christ that we will be together again in heaven. I don't want to forget the wonderful memories we shared. Trent was my best friend and still is my inspiration. We have a "forever" relationship. I continue to build new forever relationships with my family and friends, and someday I will be able to share them with him.

We are all travelers in the wilderness of this world,

and the best we can find in our travels is an honest friend.

ROBERT LOUIS STEVENSON

I THANK MY GOD
EVERY TIME I REMEMBER YOU. . . .
I HAVE YOU IN MY HEART.

PHILIPPIANS 1:3, 7 NCV

New Life

When I first lost Trent, I felt like the whole world was moving on and that I was floating outside of it, just trying to find my place. After a while, it seemed like I gently fell back to the earth, and when my feet touched the hard ground, I met Jesus there—waiting for me. After floods of tears, I trusted God with my emotions. I had no doubt He cared, and through His love I discovered who I really was. I looked at myself as if from the outside, and I saw a little girl whose life was just beginning again. When our picture-perfect lives come crashing down, the truth of God's love and promise will carry us through.

Seasons change. Seasons of life move along. Each new one draws us out of the old one. I'm coming to life again. My confession of faith is like a battle. I raise a clenched fist and declare, "Yes!"

Yes, I will fight the lies of the enemy—defeat, depression. Yes, Lord, I will be a survivor. My battle cry is "Yes!"

People who hear me echo back "Yes!" from their lives. They join me in the battle cry, and at that moment there is no misunderstanding. We choose life, love, and our Lord.

Keep Dancing!

When I'm out ministering, I move from the battle of acceptance into dance. Into worship. There is strength in that. Totally free, totally fearless. I dance like no one is watching, and I dance like everyone is watching. Because this is also my confession. I hope people go home from a Tammy Trent event and dance in their own ways. Move the chairs and the furniture! Push everything away! Make room! Give yourself space! Give yourself permission to laugh and have fun even in your circumstances. Break free. It's time to move beyond the sorrow through the hope of God's promises. His promises never fail. Never! And they will bring you back to life again.

God's invitation is compelling: "This is about us and your healing. You need Me. Here I am. I'm not going anywhere. Shut the door. Let's spend time together. Just us."

The dance is one of the few ways that two will ever learn to move as one. Trust Him with your steps. He's a great leader. Don't be afraid to follow.